T0208804

The Love Project

Volume 1: Unsinkable Spirit

GEORGINA RUTH SMITH

iUniverse, Inc.
New York   Bloomington

The Love Project
Volume 1: Unsinkable Spirit

iUniverse books may be ordered through booksellers or by contacting:

iUniverse
1663 Liberty Drive
Bloomington, IN 47403
www.iuniverse.com
1-800-Authors (1-800-288-4677)

ISBN: 978-1-4502-3573-0 (pbk)
ISBN: 978-1-4502-3574-7 (ebk)

Printed in the United States of America

iUniverse rev. date: 7/13/2010

Contents

Foreword

Everyone knows the story of the Titanic. On a cold April night in 1912 it struck an iceberg and sank in icy waters of the North Atlantic, killing over 1500 passengers making it one of the deadliest maritime disasters not caused by war in history. That an unsinkable ship could sink on her maiden voyage was an unfathomable tragedy, and one that on the surface escapes comprehension of how it could occur. But if you take a look at some of the facts, history, and story around the Titanic a clearer picture emerges.

The Titanic was built with metallurgy of steel that was found to lose its elasticity and become brittle in cold or icy water. The rivets used to hold the steel together were also found to be brittle. The rudder, although up to code was too small to turn the ship of its size effectively. The design of the main turbine and engines was such that when thrown into reverse the main turbine stopped, making the rudder less effective. The ship was travelling in an unusually windless moonless night, creating a calm flat ocean, and travelled at an excessive speed for an area known to have icebergs. The ship was designed to withstand a rupture of up to four forward compartments, and ironically if it hadn't have turned it may have only damaged the first two compartments, instead of the five that were ruptured on the side. After the impact it took over an hour for the engineers to start evacuations as they were unsure of how damaged the ship actually was. There were an insufficient number of lifeboats to save all the passengers and some didn't even get on board because they didn't believe the ship was going to sink.

The point is that any tragedy is not brought about by one failure or cataclysmic event. It is usually caused by multiple factors coinciding to fail all at the same time. And this is the story of my sister, the author of the poems in the book you are about to read. She was the girl with the unsinkable spirit and her passing was a tragedy caused by many coinciding factors.

Gina was the type of girl who was always smiling, always super silly, always having fun. She was in many ways a big kid, the type of person who would bring a stuffed animal named Monkey Jim to the Rain Forest Café for her 30th birthday. She was a kind spirit who thought nothing of helping other people before herself, the kind of person you would find buying coffee for the person in line behind her, or talking someone through a bad relationship. She helped many people through the hardest times in their lives, including me. It was her kind and forgiving nature that helped me find the woman who would be my wife. She saved my life when I got into trouble more than once. When I was a child a dog we were playing with grabbed my scarf and dragged me along the ground with me being dragged with it choking, and she ran to my parents. When I was older I accidently pulled a fire alarm in a bar thinking it was a door handle, and it was her pleading with the bouncers that kept me from being pummeled. I always thought that I was supposed to be her guardian as her big brother, but I am seeing now in many ways that she was mine. We had a shared vision of making this world a better place than it is, frustrated at the many injustices that people have to suffer. She aspired to be an artist, a singer, a songwriter, an actress, a dancer and a poet. It was her goal to make it to the Grammies and to show the world the magic of the universe through her art. I always encouraged her to follow her dreams, but her dreams were cut short.

After suffering from a deep depression and being diagnosed as bipolar she committed suicide in September of 2009. Like the story of the Titanic though her story is complex. How does someone with such a spirit get to this point? The main source of her pain and depression actually stemmed from our family breakdown 20 years prior when she was 11. Our parents divorced and our family broke apart. Our mother left us one night after we had been out of town with our father, for reasons that made sense to her, but would never make sense to child. It caused a terrible amount of pain and a sense of abandonment that we would both suffer from. We lived with our father for a year, but then my sister wanted to live with my mother because she missed her so much. I continued to live with my father, which separated us, but made us appreciate each other when we did see each other on holidays and summers instead of fighting like most siblings. We had a falling out with our mother when Gina was going off to University after which my mother never spoke to either of us, deepening that sense of loss and abandonment.

My sister never recovered from this, and her response was to lock the pain away inside. The problem is that this type of pain undealt with finds its way out in ways that are destructive. She ended up in a string of inappropriate attachments to people she couldn't have and suffered from unrequited love. She suffered from a date rape from people who were able to take advantage of her kind and trusting nature. She ended up in a relationship with a much older man who ended up physically and emotionally abusing her. I was able to get her out of this abusive relationship but this caused even more pain that she couldn't recover from. She ended up with a general anxiety disorder and depression which she took antidepressants for many years, which also from her perspective kept her from being creative and artistic. She eventually stopped taking medication, and was diagnosed many months after that as bipolar because of a manic episode. She lost her job and any means to support herself. From there she had to deal with a medical system that in my view is ineffective at dealing with people suffering from psychiatric issues. The focus seemed to be to stabilize her on powerful anti-psychotics and mood stabilizers and then get her out of the hospital. Once the doctors diagnosed her as bipolar that's all they would see. She had seen other therapists who believed that she had PTSD, but our medical system wouldn't provide her with the therapy she needed in a timely manner. It would however give her pills because this was the quick and easy thing to do. From my viewpoint this didn't work. On pills she got worse, more depressed, more dysphoric, and fell into despair. She saw a future with no hope, only pain, only suffering and only loss. She saw herself becoming a burden to me and my father and attempted to commit suicide a few times. But it didn't have to be this way. On the one hand, she may not have been bi-polar. There were many factors in her medical history that her doctors overlooked. They told me point blank that the only cause of her mania would be some type of narcotic or mental illness. But I had learned through the short time of researching the illness that there are indeed other conditions that can cause mania. One of them is Hypo-thyroidism, which can cause a host of odd symptoms many of which she had and from which our Grandfather suffered. Another is caffeine, which I only learned of recently but overuse of caffeine has been known to mimic or aggravate aspects of mental illness, and Gina was a heavy caffeine drinker.

Like the Titanic, I think that it was not any one thing that caused this tragedy, but a number of things failing at the same time, our own family history, our cultural system that leads to family breakdown, a medical system that is strained to the breaking point, doctors who don't have time to diagnose complex patients, a social services system that punishes rather than assists those who are ill, poor in-patient facilities that aggravate patients sense of despair, an over focus on medicative treatment rather than therapeutic treatment, and my own lack of understanding of how to get the system to work effectively for her. I'm not blaming the people that tried to help her; they all did the best that they could given the time and tools at their disposal. It is the system that is underneath them that needs to be fixed. Gina would want not blame, but forgiveness, but also not to let the system stands as it is, but to find ways to make it work better so that others don't have to suffer like she did. Her last act was to forgive her mother who was the original source of her pain.

Preface

Many years after the Titanic was sunk, she was found and many of her hidden treasures were unearthed and brought back to the surface. Like the Titanic, Gina had a collection of works called the Love Project. There are many poems, songs, stories and journals that she has kept over the years. Her belief was love, or lack of it to be more specific, is a root cause of many of the interpersonal problems that we have from family breakdown, crime and mental illness. Her belief was that love is all we need, and that everyone deserves to be loved, especially those who have hurt others. She believe that there was more to this world than we see with our eyes, and that in some way we are all connected together. She was extremely intuitive and felt the pain of those around her. This work of art was collected from a number of poems that she wrote in the last 9 months of her life through journals that she kept throughout her entire experience with mental illness and breakdown. I have read through these journals and transcribed, organized, and edited the poems. I have unearthed these treasures for you.

This book is not the last of her works, but the beginning. She left more than fifty journals of which this collection has only scratched the surface. I have organized this work by what she would have seen as the stages of love and loss. Starting with Hope, resulting in Love, driving a deep Longing, leading to Fear & Anger, causing Pain, and ending in Despair.

Acknowledgement

I'd like to thank my father, who in raising me and working so diligently to try and save my sister taught me that the true meaning of love is sacrifice. It was the effortless way in which my father put my needs before his, and put others needs before his own that made the difference in my life. He taught me the meaning of honour only through his example. I'd also like to thank my mother, who although the source of our pain, suffers from a pain all her own before and after what happened to my sister, and who although bears some responsibility for her state, this responsibility is shared by those who shaped her, and by me. She tried the best given the tools, time, and circumstances that her life provided for her. My sister and I having been raised in two different environments serve as a case study of the difference that love brings in our end development and state, and this collection of works would not have been possible without either of them.

Dedication

"*A society* is ultimately *judged by how it treats* its weakest and most vulnerable members"

Anonymous.

This book is written for them.

Hope

"Life and all its turns, you can only make something if dealt the right cards, tomorrow should tell."

Gina R. Smith

"One can never change the past, only the hold that it has on you. Awaken sleeping beauty, we are the hero of our own journey."

Gina R. Smith

Millennium Project
1999?

Once upon a time,
there was a girl who was
born to LIVE, and to tell
the Truth. She knew this, and
so followed every path that she
was supposed to take. Sometimes
life was downright glorious and
sometimes it was not. Sometimes
people liked what she had to say
and sometimes they didn't. And some-
times this girl liked what she had
to say and sometimes she didn't.
What this girl is trying to say is
that she knew that she was meant
to be in The Millennium Project
whether "come hell or high water".
So, she embraced the challenges
currently during her life and tried
to learn from them and to give to
and take from the moment what she
was meant to. And sometimes, she
discovers Great and wonderful things.
This time around, she discovered a
Wise Man who had an even greater
Truth to tell, and that man, being
You...

Time is Precious
Mar 2009

time is precious and so is life too
I just want there to be love
and not have my values construed

keeping faith with the change
will bring that piece of mind
the longing of life
and the will to survive

knowing I've got a few more steps to go
I'll find my way to the world I know
knowing I've got a few more steps to go
I'll conquer my fears and never let go
never let go of who I am
I'm more than just someone
I've got so much in my mind
so much to give so much to show
I'll never let go of who I truly am
I'm more than just a victim
I've got a soul that wants to grow
I'll never let go
never let go of who I am.

Open Your Eyes
Apr 21, 2009

Open your eyes, truth beware
I feel your words, I know you're there
you are my friend, the light that I see
Suddenly everything is shining on me

Profound and Wise we pierce hearts with eyes
that are too young to see haunting cries.
knowing what's right and knowing what's wrong
Words match songs what's gone on too long

Brighter than day, darker than night
You just need to believe that I am your light
Colours that fade get charged again
You lay me down and I say Amen

We stick together through thickest snakes skin.
It's the only way to breathe again
Living through truth you became aware
Believing there is beauty and magic Everywhere

Trees that sway, animals that walk
Listening to the words of people's talk
Spinning round and round sound keeps me warm.
Because it shines Love in during and after the storm

Calming and free truth is plain to see
Took so long to see that it comforts me
I can help you and you can help me
This is a truth I want the world to see

Love is magic Love is always there,
if we give it a chance there's nothing to spare.

Eyes spread wide with wonder and with awe
The power that lies within us all, our mind
& spa... it is mind that sees.. and the hearts
that feel, for they both take part in planting the seeds.

We are all magic because we are all full of love.
Shooting down from the stars and planets above.
Love is here... love can be there...
What I've learned... Love is and can be anywhere...

Cathartic Release
Mar 2009

I knew I kept walking for more
reasons than I knew
I know I kept walking because of you
Thankful with grace
smile on my face
and tears of joy
Cathartic release is what I've been wishing for
each day and moment you have
something new to show me
and I am truly amazed.
I know I will be alone once the anxiety
is gone. I pray for that day, when
I truly am ok it's what I've wanted
thank you for pushing me to take that final fall
forgive me if I stopped believing
I really am now seeing
how you've loved me all along
I hope I get to sing this song
here I am looking for it and it is there
I am in awe it feels like a dream.

Fighting the Urge
Mar 30, 2009

Fighting the urge to eat
cause I want our eyes to meet
locked in an embrace
I really miss your face.

Never Said Goodbye
Apr 7, 2009

I never said goodbye
she must have known I would stay
You'll never see me again.
Life is now or never
forever never slow me down.

You Must Be Here
Apr 14, 2009

I feel cold you must be here
you are always here I know now
all of you come and go anytime
you like ok? My home is
your home.

Wake up smell the spirits
lingering sweet scents of spring
awakening our senses to
the sound of everything.

Time for Peace
Apr 21, 2009

God, it is time for peace, it
is time for love all because
I found the light within and
above profound are my thanks
to the beauty and Awe
I won't let you down with my talents so raw
Time to rock, time to Roll, I feel the
Comfort of you all!

A Little Pink
Apr 21, 2009

Put a little pink on your sleeve
It reminds you to breathe
put a little pink in the air
it reminds to see
put a little pink where it hurts
it'll remind you of peace
Put a little pink in your soul
it'll remind you to feel
Put a little pink in your face
it reminds you to smile.
Put a little pink in your toes
to remind you to dance, with wind in your hair.
with all of the love to spare.

And We're Trying Again
Apr 24, 2009

Keep on trying
keep on trucking till our heart gets it right
till there's nothing left to fight
Games turn to dreams
rivers down to streams
Joy becomes bliss
A magical rainbow kiss
Shed from old skin
Smiling eyes that begin
Seeing stars through clouds
hearts that beat
Away from defeat
the moon is high
Full of delight
The sun shines smiles
through veins of love
thankful to those
Who shine from above
mystery lies in
misery we see
unraveling the cord
to set us free.

Sometimes you
just gotta say
you give in
if only for one
day, so you can
get it right
mistakes are ok
it is ok
everything is all right.

Stories Told
May 13, 2009

Stories told of a life far away
Bring dreams to life
where mysteries lay
I close my eyes to see the truth
and listen to the whispers
and beautiful sounds
loving and touching
from soul to soul.

Lift Up My Feet
May 14, 2009

The wind keeps pushing me to lift up my feet
giving in to eat to make our eyes meet
helpless and scared afraid to say a thing
not wanting to cry and face the pain I'm in
Driven with love, driven with desire
focused on the dream, so real it seems
Want to leave this scary place
want to see my happy face
To go play in the sun, to know that we have won.

Life And Love
May 15, 2009

Tired of these walls
that surround my loving heart
Finding who I am
has been a blessed start
Smiling has begun to untie
those knarly knots
letting out that anger
to let out all that fear
but anxious to see
the very best of me
believing we are good
will set our heart and mind free
eyes that do see
every breath around
is beauty to my soul
and colours I surround
calming, flowing energy
begins to raise up from within
Knowing we are found
Letting love poureth in
I learn to love myself
gourmet dessert at its best
Tasty and delicious
A life that's full of zest
Funny how it seems
that we held back for way too long
Funny now I see
Every moment is a song
breathing life inside
is the answer to our soul
never lost again
We stick to our new goal

Feels so good to know
that we are here
Freedom is now here
For crying all those tears
We have found our home
Sent from up above
Wishes and Dreams
Because God is really love
Hard to explain
how it all began
But knowing we are love
Wondering why we ever ran.
Every magic moment
is really life that's all around
Life and love are all that really matters
it keeps us on solid ground
Yet soaring to the sky
Thou our hearts and minds
Believing we are all special
That we all are one of a kind.

Glistening Raindrops
May 18th, 2009

Raindrops glisten in the sparkly air
Twirling in front of my face
Your smell lingers a wondrous taste

Hearing sound from afar
I look around I see new stars
From a distance, in night and sky

Colliding with a force
Greater than this earth we walk upon
they melt and yonder in existence.

We march along, we march ahead
We see it all laid out
We see what we are made of

Here is goes, the whistle blows,
Speaking volumes, speaking truths
We come together, we call a truce.

War is over and we all rejoice
Never had we heard, they said
Such a wondrous angelic voice

I wonder who they mean
I look from left to right
I see all their faces looking right at me

Oh I say Oh my Oh my
Laughing, head tilting I begin
to sing my song and finally grin

Magical and beautiful
The skeptics all agree, they all believe
because I shon light on you and me.

Time is come, now it is the time
for all of us to dance, to sing
It's time for bells at last to chime.

The peace we feel lets us now heal
We have had our say
We know it is here to stay.

Nothing to be Afraid of
May 19, 2009

Nothing to be afraid of
We think of what we love
about ourselves, about the world
We all can be free
Just letting go of past
worries, troubles, pain
Will bring us love
and it is our minds we gain
No more running
No more pain
Only comfort and joy
Only true love
and happiness
Real tears we long to cry
To heal us in our minds
So another moment
So another to time
Another day of blessings
Another day of love
Another day of love
Another day of love.

Alone is not a Place
May 19, 2009

Alone is not a place that I want to be
For very long
Only sometimes when I need to think
about our world
how much it stinks
and needs to be saved
how much we really need
to make some changes
alone is a time of self reflection
A time for peace
A time for rest
Alone is a moment when you realize
how blessed you are
to be alive in this world
a moment of bliss
Like a star shined kiss.
Alone is a place inside our hearts
to feel, to love
to cherish always
and to hold onto our hearts
to keep love together
never apart...

Fire Branches Out
May 19, 2009

Fire branches out
into rivers beyond
water to the flame
only smoke lingers
in the air
Lost and tired
we come round once
again
Into a new reality
wondrous, splendid, clean
waking is reliving
it is worth
damn living
breathing in the
new air
rejoicing all that
is really there
serenity at last
we clap our hands
together
together we have
passed.

Smiles That Are Faded
May 19, 2009

Smiles that are faded
find their sun again
Looking in the puddles
that engulf the state
you are in
surprises trickle in
to tickle you with
Delight
All because you
put up
One hell of a fight
Nothing left to say
except that you are
now ok.
Blessings turned inwards
Really do mark the day
Rewarded for your strength

those smiles lasting years
All because you chose
to face all your worst fears
chaos turned to order
Balance found within
make you smile brighter
with a new life to begin.

Sweeping up the cobwebs
of all that used to be
you chose your freedom
you chose to be able
to be a bird, to fly free

Smiles bring in laughter
of painful memories stored away
new life has begun
it started with Today.

Peaceful and calming
our minds now at ease
let love in our hearts
it is the perfect kind of start

Seeing My Face
May 21, 2009

Seeing my face
not a stranger
it's you I see
I'm seeing me
feels so good to
see my own smile
reflecting back
hadn't seen in awhile
pretty and fun
Days in the sun
are coming back
It's true, it's a fact
carefree I will be
I will just be me
smiling around
glad I am found...

The Skin I am in
May 21, 2009

The skin I am in
really lets me grow
The skin I am in
really lets me glow
The skin I am in
really lets me know

Forever I am kind
and no longer blind
happiness starts
with loving your own heart

Finding the words
that always seem hard to say
Finding the rhythm
in my heart I stay

Swaying to the music
Saying in the wind
Swaying with my soul
Praying from my toes

I love to laugh
I really love to sing
I can feel the air
propelling my sacred wings

I now take flight
and off to a new day
full of wonder
full of many, many
wonderful things....

So Low, So High
May 22, 2009

Feeling low so that I can feel high
is a result of not loving yourself inside
But with self love comes that natural
high
You will do anything to get it
it's worth the buy
traveled so long to get here today
Found out I have a lot to say
Fears and Demons you used to see
turn to dust, you can clear it away

Here I am golden and pure
I know I've made it
it's now so clear

When you believe you invest in yourself
You take the time to see yourself
you fight and try you are amazing
Just believe that I am here.

Nothing to Fear
May 22, 2009

Nothing to fear and nothing to hide
Everyone loves you, you are one of a kind
Sweet and pure like honey from a bee
The world starts smiling as you begin to see

Inside you are precious you know that you are
inside your heart you know you're a star
here today and always forever
you started this journey you are so clever

Champions rise and beg to differ
you steal the thunder because you miss her
Here we go, it's time to go home
Just say I love you and it will be ....

Life is a Gift
May 22, 2009

Life is a gift
not to be wasted
we are all precious
if we just believe
Life is here now
so let's enjoy
every moment that
we have to just be
to be alive is life
To love is to live
To breathe is to live
To sing is my life

It's Time to Come In.
May 22, 2009

It's time to come in
It's time to shine
It's time to live
It's time for now
It's all about the moments
of each and every day

Loving each moment
that we are truly our self
It's all about how we feel inside
It's all about loving ourselves

Doing what's best
to make ourselves whole
Doing what's best
To nourish our souls

We can make our dreams
Come to life
by trusting our heart
That's where we start

The time is now
not yesterday
Not tomorrow
but now.

Rainbow
May 30, 2009

Rainbow so bright
you give me my light
I watch with awe
so glorious are thee
it makes me wonder
how I could not see
the colours so bright
give me warmth tonight
for what I see
is the best in me
Magical and beautiful
each colour tells a story
of life here and then
now and before
not blinded but golden
it matches the sun
wondrous summer
fun has begun
rainbow so bright
you are my light

Gifts of Love
May 31, 2009

Gifts of the future
aren't always wrapped in bows
they come in voices
from people you know

unwrapping the love
between open arms
setting in the love
that is so warm

Summer breezes wisp through the air
circling your soul
moving through your hair

Gifts are the present
that are coloured inside
cherished forever
in calm peace of mind

Smiles abound
frowns disappear
the love from people
keep the world so clear.

Look to the Sky
May 31, 2009

Look to the sky
Don't even ask why
just take it as is
and leave the stars
who are wise
to summon my soul
and turn me whole
I love to see them
they bring me joy
remind me of times
of past and now.

Running and Falling
May 31, 2009

Running and Falling
no way to live
Facing the fear
and crying the tears
letting people in
to warm your heart
looking within
a good place to start
up in the air
we fly to the sky
eagles that soar
and lions that roar

Feeling so good
amazing it seems
life is a miracle
that's how it seems

twisted and turning
to find the right way
yearning to find
what we need to stay

Feeling the start
of something wonderful
and new

Feeling your heart
as you once know

Boiling to the Point
Jun 2, 2009

Boiling to the point
tired within
Swirling to escape
masks hide the pain

Leaves to the ground
your warmth gives me sound

Swaying with the wind
to let our lives begin

Praying to the stars
wishing what will be

God has given
the light in me

Prayers turned to whispers
dreams turned to song

To reveal all the truth
we've known all along

Written in the sky
a song to sing
hearts do not lie
and do not question why

Soft as the spring
cool like the fall
trembling inside
our fragile minds

Stronger with the
winter
and warmed by
summer song

We change like
the weather
to see us
start again

Stones in our
minds
fall to the ground
clear water
springs
bring love
within.

Clouds with Bubbles
Jun 3, 2009

Clouds with bubbles
pop away in the air
Sailing away
through blue clean air

Falling through rivers
upwards the stream
falling through rivers
downward the stream

Picking on Love
Jun 5, 2009

Picking on hate
picking on love
we keep on searching
from above
Guiding us through
to find our hearts
knowing that we
are never apart
growing tall
even though we
feel small

feeling the earth
feeding the sky
we don't stop to
question why
walking ahead
to move back time
we end the war
we end the crime
looking around
to see all who's
there
We see ourselves
we become aware

Gracious Glorious
Jun 10, 2009

Gracious Glorious
blessed are thee
for following my way
to those I teach today
May I grant you
one special wish
to have all your crystals
in one single dish
let them be spread
so that others may see
the miracles I show you
with wonder and glee
you need to believe
you know that it is right
I am your candle
I am your light
put down those
darkened thoughts
pick up clouds from
the sky instead
Dream that thou are
holy
Dream that you are not
dead
Believe in your soul
Believe in my heart
I wish you sweet dreams
this very special night.

Smoke Gathers
Jun 15, 2009

Smoke gathers within
trapped beneath the doors
lies within the seen
rays of colour
bursting forth
to set sights high
to soar above what
once was lost
grasping to the strings
of a broken heart
indeed
shadows fall away
someone new emerges
it is the old
but flames anew
show the world
the triumph
of finding
the I that is who

Time, Time, Time
June 17th, 2009

Time is here
I believe it is true
to find oneself
and to start anew
time can heal
seasons can change
light within
can radiate all around
love is special
time is today
not yesterday
time is of present
to change the past
time is of now
to change the future
time has colours
like that of rainbows
that fall from the sky
time, time, time
love, love, love
today, today, today...

Time to Heal
Jun 17th, 2009

Coming around seeing the bend
take time to heal
take time to mend
we all see the truth
lying within
we all see the colours
rising within
surmounting our fears
we win the war
we know where we're going
and we're going far...

Bountiful Beauty
Jun 20th, 2009

Bountiful beauty
locked up in chains
haste my friends
do not fear
the door will be opened
and bright lights do
appear
suddenly, miraculously
we all see the light
shining within
so bright we are
all in glow of
the effect of the
star we have all
been longing to
see. That is a dream
we all need to see.

Lost Finding Home
Jun 28th, 2009

Lost finding home
counting the seconds
until I see the light
where I belong
where I long to be
no more tears
no more pain
just peace inside
happiness too
smiles abound
gone are the frowns
gone is the medicated confusion
of perfect minds
destroyed
by drugs and rage of it all
Lights I do
crave, music
I do hear
no same old
just brand new
days with
sand on the beach
and sun in my
hair, that is
peace to me.

Feelings of Hope
Jul 4, 2009

Feelings of hope
Found at the
end of the rope
We all find
a way to
get through our pain
we hide we run
we find all the fun
waiting for us
underneath the sun
stories all told
some young some old
but we all have a
reason to cry or
to laugh
to feel is important
in order to reach
our goals
we need to connect
feel the vibration of
love radiating from
our souls.

Caring Heart Bleeds
Jul 12, 2009

My caring heart bleeds for all
So we came together in harmony
where we all see the same
twinkles in the stars
and sun no matter where we go
I long for us all to see
Happiness and love as
the ultimate goal.

Round and Round
Jul 14th, 2009

round and round and round we go
looking for answers to ease the flow
mountains to climb
trees to watch
people to talk
we learn to walk
finding our way
through puddles of rain
wonder why we were ever stained
love in our hearts we do not part
crying for each other
to change the doomed weather
together we blow
in harmony we flow

Rising Steam
Aug 25, 2009

Steam a rising
wind blowing in
flowers are fatigued
hair strangled in
so far away it seems
That peace had on the night
Train had brought in
a girl with a deep sense of fright
world below sky
thunder pounding in
shaking from the heavens
please let the light in
too much of the sea
and not enough land
we are to bring love
if we can find the
space within
Dreaming of the
past and all
that can really be
Turn away the
ocean unveil
the new me
waiting for so long
sky no longer overcast
look over your shoulder
to the ghosts of
years past.

Bringing Around Hope
Sept 18, 2009

Bringing around
the time for change
one we all hope for
one we all crave
it's insane to think
we may have known
all along
insane to think we
can all get along
a world of peace
a world of love
brought together
we are all one
not just a story
but in fact a truth
I want to shout it
aloud from roof
to roof
we all can see
with one simple
mind
love brings us
together
we are all
one of a kind.

Love

"Sometimes courage takes you places you don't want to go, but you go cause you know you have to."

Gina R. Smith

"The heart has many countless beats that fall between the stars."
"It's really scary what I've written, I guess I must have been smitten."

Don't Keep Me Hidden
Feb, 2009

If you love me don't keep me hidden behind a wall
cause this has what's caused me to fall
cherish me and love me
really show you care for me
that is what will set me free
someone who really understands and loves me
because I know me, I love me, it's all about me

Wanted Love
Mar, 2009

Maybe if I turned gay I'd find love that way
but I know that is wrong because I am strong
one day soon I'll find that love I bet
one day soon all my needs will be met
so wired how the brain works - I wanted love so
badly I was willing to be gay when I'm not?
She cared. I think that was a huge trigger pot.

Love Is All We Really Need
Mar 2009

Love is all what we really need
not lies and deceit not hatred and greed
love keeps us alive breathing for air
it keeps us going through all the despair

Rough times make us strong
they don't make us wrong
we need love in our hearts
and that's where it starts

It feels so good to have someone who cares
to hold you tight through all the wear and tear
to feel secure to know that everything's all right
to be able to sleep with sweet dreams every night

No nightmares no screams not ripped at the seams
love will keep us strong through rivers and streams
love is all we really need what we really do need
family and friends and the pets that we feed.

A breath of fresh air like the early morning spring
knots stay untied and as straight as string
love is all what we all really need
it keeps us from crumbling to the ground on our knees
above it all love will get us through it all.

Falling
Apr 12, 2009

I can feel myself falling
gently now God
No longer scared of what
may be.
I've learned my lessons
about love and faith
Money and dreams
I want to show the
world all that I see I seen
I want to show the world
What I can be
I want to love all the world
and have that love
shine back at me.

Everything
Apr 12, 2009

I felt my
heart and
gave it stars

The moon
shines
back its
love to me

All I can
be shines
brightly
I can
barely
see
but I feel
it all
I feel
everything

Surged with
storm
driven by
desire I
Mean everything
to me.

So Pretty so
serene my
thoughts are
changing about
everything I've

seen

Pure like the
sun I see it's
face in me
hope is its
light shining
down on me
dreams are the
shape its
turning out to be
its colours give
me faith that
I am landing
and falling safely
looking right
at me it is
cradling me
beaming its light
so I can sleep
peacefully.

Mothers
May 10, 2009

Mothers

Mothers are special, mothers are kind
Together we are one, we are wild and free
Love like no other, even more than a brother
Together we live in Harmony.
When you don't have the time but you do have the LOVE
You will do anything to set your Heart free
You will remember your Mother, how precious she is
For she gave you life, she gave you your memories
Never to be forgotten, Never to be unloved,
the Bond between a Mother and a Child
can never be unleashed
If she is not around but she is in your Heart and Soul
Please tell her that before it's too late or you will never know...
A smile and a laugh, good times you once had
CAN be brought back with three simple words of I LOVE thee.
Your are who you are because of your Mother,
something that should never be taken for granted, or your dreams,
your life, will never be planted.
A Mother's touch, her comfort and her smile, are what a child craves,
forever and a mile. As we grow, the LOVE never goes away.
For LOVE is something that will always stay.
the Bond is glued; never untied running shoes.
So on this Mother's Day, a lesson to us all, please thank your Mothers,
TELL them, I LOVE You!
Do Whatever it takes to make her Smile, for it is Her day and she
deserves to feel Special,
to KNOW that she IS LOVED.
LOVE is THE most Powerful thing in the World, nothing can take
that away...
Unless you are left Unloved, it can destroy it all, we Have to LOVE
Ourselves too!

A Story We All Know
May 2009

too hard to handle
in a world that's so cold
wanting to be one way
in a story that's told

it run so deep
through all of my veins
truth in the story
that is centuries old

that love is what makes
the world go round
not paper bills
not false advertising

but love that makes
us move to our feet
it has a craving
keeps out the defeat

a story we all know
so very well indeed
all in truth
all in speed

not too hot to touch
but warmth in our souls
love can bring us
up on our toes

let's get together
all and one

and rise above
the warm shining sun

to see new days
that lie straight ahead
lets hold on tight
and grab love instead

Together
May 14, 2009

One last move so the story goes
to break me down and forget all my woes
Sun to the east, Sun to the West
Grieving and receiving, loving till the end.
Family and Friends all the people I do meet
Have come here together to lift me off my feet.
Into the new world where I do belong
Heaven here on Earth, a smile and a song.
Craving the sweet sound, feeling my heart pound.
Never to be alone, we have found our loving home.
Hugs, laughter, tears, we've waited for so long
Fearless and Ferocious, never do we back down
Together we do fall
Together we Love all
Never did I suspect
These days would heal us all
Funny now how it seems
Why fears took our way
But look at all that's written
We triumphed with our say
Laughing in between, seeing the dotted lines
Wondering how on Earth
We had been forever blind
Feels so good to know
that everyone is here
To ground me in my heart
and cry those bitten tears
Here and Now, then and future be
Grabbing on to Love
so that we can see
Bookshelves Full at last
with stories old and new

Take us to new dimensions
writing our own cries
We smile in the end
We smile as of right now
We enjoy the every second
And all we say is wow....

Love Is Here to Stay
May 18, 2009

Why do we all
get scared to face our fears
If we just take a look
of what's inside
We see who is there
There is nothing to hide
We see our chance
to be free again
We see ourselves
like we've never seen
We all become thankful
For the life that is inside
The sun shines in brightly
We feel the comfort
The peace of who we are
We all come together
We are all together friends.
We are all together lovers
We are all one piece of mind
I look at myself and
find that I love myself inside.
For true beauty
true happiness
true love
is being who we are
and loving what we
have accomplished
and what will be
accomplished in our lifetime
To love ourselves is to
love others
we crave the love inside

Love does bring the peace
Love brings our peace of mind
Today is love, always in our hearts
Love is here to stay
Love is the final say
We grow, we love
We love we grow
We look to the sky
and feel our soul glow
happiness is set
happiness is won
The game is over
The game is done.

Song for Dad
May 2009

dreams are nothing if you are not alive
feels like my world is crashing down

this is a song for my dad
He's always there when I am sad
when nothing goes right
and everything is wrong
These are my words
why don't you sing along
where would I be without your love
Money is nothing
without your smile.

You are a dream to me
now I am flying so free
the kind of person
I strive to be
Love in your heart
a smile that beams
you bring me love
gone are my tears

Forever is a word
I like to use whenever
I'm blue I think of you

Lying in blood
you wipe me clean
I see my life like
I've never seen

the rebel in me is

because of you
I take risks all
because of you

I follow my heart
because I follow yours
beating so loud like
that of a drum

happy days
you always
bring I think
of you and
I love to sing
I want to sing
I die to sing.

Father Knows Best
May 21, 2009

Father knows best
or so they always say
He is always there
He is always here to stay

He sees me when I cry
He sees me when I laugh
He sees me in my skin
He sees where I begin

Loving and gentle
patient and kind
Thee love from my Father
Brings me peace of mind

Glad Father is here
Glad Father is there
Glad for the Love I feel
when I am with my loving Father

No matter what I do
no matter what I say
I always have my father
in my heart you stay

Forever in my heart
Forever in my mind
Forever in my smile
You've been here all the while

I love to see your face
brighten up each day I see

that once again I'm finding
how much I do love me.

Fathers teach us love
Fathers teach us many things
to always love your Father
to know that he is there.

I thank him for my life
I thank him for my soul
I thank God that he is here
My mind is so much clear

Father does know best
For he is one of a kind
I truly love my Father
Always and now
I love my dearest Father

Too Hard to Handle
May 25, 2009

Too hard to handle
in a world that's so cold
wanting to be one way
in a story that's told

it runs so deep
through all of my veins
truth in the story
that is centuries old

that love is what makes the world go round
not paper bills
not false advertising

But love that makes
us move to our feet
it has a craving
keeps out the defeat

A story we all know
so very well indeed
All in truth
All in speed

Not too hot to touch
but warmth in our souls
Love can bring us
up on our toes

Let's get together
all and one
and rise above

the warm shining sun

To see new days
that lie straight ahead
let's hold on tight
and grasp love instead.

Hugs
May 25, 2009

Hugs are special
hugs bring warmth
they connect us together
They show the love

We need touch
in order to grow
We need each other
We need us all

We all need love
We all need faith
We all need to heal
We all need a smile

It's been a while
that I've felt really
loved
but today it is shining
from above.

My Brother
May 25, 2009

My brother is my friend
He is always there
to lend a helping hand

He listens when I talk
he hears the things
I have to say

He hugs me when I cry
Even when
I really don't know why

My brother is the best
friend I've ever had
he is the one; for that I am glad

I love my brother
for always being there
I love my brother
because he cares.

My Sister
May 25, 2009

My sister is sweet
She teaches me things
I do not yet know

She really does help me
to live and to grow
I give thanks, I bestow

My sister is great
for just being there
When I am troubled

She loves me and I love here
I need her, she needs me
Because we are family

Memories of old
memories of new
my sister is my friend
always and now

I love my sister
for smiles we share
I love my sister
I really do care

Catching the Sand
Jun 6, 2009

Catching the sand
between our toes
talking of stories
no one knows

trying to get
them to listen

to what I've seen
where I've been
I know others
have come before
they have all
marched through the door

they know what's there
I know what's there
all of the others
just wait and stare
we shine and we listen
to the songs of the past
we try to live to make it last
crying to be different
crying to be free
crying to shout out
what we really need
love inside and from above
love outside comes
roaring in.

Some Days Are Hard
June 10th, 2009

Some days are hard
yet some such a dream
you come to realize
it is what you seem

One day you're fine
one day you scream
and in the end
it's all just a dream

Never really happened
never really occurred
but love held you together
love showed you the dream

We're put here together
to be one as all
put here together
in love as a dream

this way and that
front forth and back
to times we had
to time we will have

Was it all real
was it all a dream
What did we learn
What did we bring

Smiles and laughter
are the ending

it seems

hugs and surprises
are what
happiness means
like flowers that grow
our colours shine too
scents of reminders
of what we once
knew.

When You Don't See Hope
Aug 25, 2009

Hard
When you don't see hope
only shadows in between
you don't want to turn
or fear what you'll live
blackened by dust
and washed by the rain
people all wonder
what made you stained
comforted by sound
comforted by touch
you begin to question
what you are really made of
people that care can
turn it all around
showing you care
can create sound above
the love we feel and
the love that we get
lets us remember
and helps us to forget
hugs and laughter
crying and tears
help to combat
all of those fears

Beautiful Love
Sept 8, 2009

A beautiful love
a beautiful spirit
haunted by her soul
searching within
to really know
overcast shadows
that loom around
her heart
she's trying to fight
them
trying to reach her true soul
one way goes this way
the other way goes that way
conflicted by sorrow
self hatred and doubt
wants the world to
know
what she is all about
the love within
she wants to scream and shout.

Love Questions Why
Sept 10, 1009

Love Love
we question why
we look around
not seeing who is there
we go each day
not really knowing
what we are doing here
moments go by
clouds float by
but no one seems
to notice
the magic in
the air
the way
the world smells
everyone caught
up in a swirl
of disbelief
to the reality
that is really
there
what do we
see
pain, agony
when joy is
just in the
blink of an eye
no more questions
why

Grab Love While You Can
Sept 19, 2009

Grab it while you can
all the love you have
you see it in the trees
you feel it in the air
surrender to your soul
that's how you'll know
Love is there
to be kind
to those who wait
standing at the gate
grab it while you can.
we all need it
all the fear you
have
and throw it all
away
its shadows
haunt the night
burning out your
light
Love is there to
be your friend
God is waiting for
you on the other
side of the gate.

Longing

"I long for the days of cherished sun, where all I knew was happiness and fun."

Gina R. Smith

Don't You Feel The Same?
2008

Lost in worry you won't even glance my way
I'm finding it hard to believe that you don't feel the same way
Though why would you when I sulk and cry
all I wish is that you wouldn't lie
feeling so strong I don't know what to do
Weakening by day yet my love for you still grows
tired of waiting losing all sense of life
can barely smile or move
I need to be able to move on if you don't feel the same way
wish I could smile your way just so you'd know
I want to be together all I want is you

Sitting in Silence
Dec 24, 2008

I know I love you why can't I tell you
I'm sitting here silent in the lights
I try to fight it. Makes me feel worse
I can't imagine how you must be feeling too.

Find the New Rhythm
Dec 24, 2008

I can only look outside and hope the sky is bright
I've got no hunger pains tonight
my heart is melting and my eyes have dried with tears
wanting to be with you wondering if it's ok
the notes bring comfort to the churning in my stomach
but only for a minute until the sound fades away
my fingers are aching to play and take your pain away
anything I touch right now feels like velvet on my skin
smooth & soft I want this love to begin
my heart feels weird like it's all out of
beat like I'm a new dancer with two left feet
Trying to find the rhythm & emotion
that makes my heart sing
I wish that I could know you
I wish that you know me please understand me
I'm crying to be free
your eyes are like sugar sweeter than I've ever had.

Only a Kid
Mar 2009

I was only 11
I was only a kid
all I keep wondering
is what I did.

Kept sobbing why why why why
why did you leave us why???
That wasn't fair
I think I fell on a chair

Why did you leave? You just left us to grieve
sobbing all night rubbing tears on my sleeve
so much pain that I had never felt
dreams were shattered you made my heart melt
ripped at the seams and torn all apart
you left as along you left us to scream
my heart full of tears that won't wash away
what life would I have had if you had stayed

I'm angry at you for leaving us that day
we had loving hearts buy you turned away
I'm angry at you I deserve my say
or I'll be stuck here forever it won't go away

So I'm letting go goodbye and goodnight
I'll always remember our kisses goodnight
I'll see you one day if it's meant to be
but for now letting go goodbye and goodnight.

God's Worst Curse
Mar 12, 2009

Two hours of crying is not enough the page is stained with tears
that's how much my life has been damaged by fears
my life has been hard but this is much worse
not being loved by you was God's worst curse

but I know I'll be in a much better place
I'll still check in just in case
we all have our reasons we have to go on our way
God's greatest gift to teach us to pray

To believe in our hearts and to always be kind
so that all our fears don't get trapped inside
To love and to give to forget and forgive
that is how we can only live.

Scared I'll Forget You
Mar 2009

I wish to thank all those who have crossed my path
because step by step is what led me to crash
if this had not been I would not see the light in front of me
I would never be able to let myself free

we're going to do it again and again until we
get it right I will never end the fight
Life is worth living I've wanted it all along
I've always just wanted to sing my songs

I don't forget you I'm so scared I will
cause that will leave me standing still
never have I been so afraid
I'll hold on to the memories with all my will.

I thank you always from the bottom of my heart
you let me sing you let me shout
you let me free to be me
that's what this is all about

You were the one who just let me be
no matter how different you always loved me
I miss you so much but I want to be free
I want to be the person I had chosen to be

Why do I have to let her go
I love her so much
it hurts so much

Mom I love you I need to let you go
why did you leave
it hurts sooo much I don't want to grieve

I wish I had more pictures so I won't forget your face
it's always brought me comfort when I didn't feel safe
but when I came back when I was 12 you were not the same
Ever since that day everything had changed
But I want my life back my songs and my
dreams and I need to grow up not haunted by your steam.

I'll still be the same ol'me just stronger
and wiser and more womanly
I know you tried your hardest to teach me
what you know
but deep down inside you were hit with an arrow

I hope one day you'll come back to me
and see the girl you taught me to be
a song in my heart a smile on my sleeve
arms wide open for love to receive

Saying Goodbye is Hard
Mar 17, 2009

Looking at the picture had started crying in the bath
My heart is sad as I write this now
saying goodbye is one of the hardest things
a heart could ever know
breathing for air gets harder to do
I just feel like laying here in my own world
the sadness is real which I don't want to feel
it hurts to the core but I want more
dying to live and gasping for air
but I am coming back, would beware
My heart it is melting with bad memories
Just pumping with these that will always last
the words have no rhyme but they are all mine
Trying to breathe my heart so sad
letting go of my mother I knew I once had
Tears stain my pillow as they escape from
my face laying here still all in our place
Each tear says goodbye no longer asks why
just falls through the air like raindrops from the sky
rainbows are shining and planets are aligning
Things may change like the seasons I love
birds fly ahead and protect me above
I am saying goodbye with the heart
full of tears
the memories will take me through all
of the years.

I have to not care what others think
I have to reach for the sky as high as I can
love every moment of the air that I breathe
Drive to the mountains the highest point I can stand

Divine right action is always taking place
in my life. Only good comes from each experience
It is safe to grow up.
Denying your own power
The world is safe and friendly I am
safe I am at peace with life.

I have the strength power and skill to
digest whatever comes my way

Alone Because of You
Mar 2009

I've been so conflicted on how to get love right
how to get everything right
life & my dreams
the nightmares I scream
tears and the pain
all those who I've blamed
I needed to look deeper
to see the bigger picture
The Love Project has been the story of it all
the story of my life
that has caused me so much strife
I'm alone because of you
because I finally fell to my knees
cried for the help I so desperately needed
let myself fall right over the edge
before I let myself off of the ledge
The Love Project is all because of you
it was all inside
I always knew
love will make me new
all my love for you
you let me see the darkest dark I have ever seen
so I could see all the light that lay between
the rain turning dry with the air that I need
love mending my heart before it bleeds

Having my Say
Mar 20, 2009

You may call me names
but I won't go away
I've waited much too long
to have my say

Just laying drifting away in my own head
trying to figure it all out so I come out ahead
blissful colours and radiant sun
bring me home together we are one

Ahead of our time wise beyond our years
we find why we've laid in puddles of our tears
The signs have all been written
by the stars that lay above

No longer dreaming I lay wide awake
yearning to hear that sound
that will play softly in my ear
to spread joy in what I've found

Can't Find You
Mar 25, 2009

I can't find you all alone on my own
but I want to go home
I can see what others don't
I can see your ghost
I can feel what others feel
but I can't find you.

She's Not Coming Back
Mar 30, 2009

It's only this hard
it only hurts this much
because of how much
I really do love you

But if I don't say goodbye
now, I will waste away
and the world will say
wow that's such a shame

I'd like to find peace
so that I may sleep
I'd like to find peace
so that I may sing

I'm angry that it has to be this way
but deep in my heart I know, it's the only way

Precious you are and so am I
I will keep you in mind as I perform
knowing you are there, somewhere watching
I'll make you proud just wait and see

I'm letting you go, all of you
letting go of anger, letting go of hurt
letting in the sun, letting in the love
I'm letting in my every own heart

That girl is here with the universal dreams
She's worked so heard she knows where she's been.

Glad to be alive she almost died

Grateful to all who let her begin
Smiles in her eyes, songs in her heart
The tears and gone from all the years apart

Never again will she look in the mirror
and see someone who's scared and full of fear.

The pain, so real, felt more than the rest
But she kept holding on because she is truly the best.
My story so far, let's sees where it goes
may it never stop; only God knows.

She's gone, it's over, she's not coming back
it truly is real I have to face that fear
I look over the edge and I watch her fall
along with my anger from when I was small

Hardly feels real, hope I'll be all right
just want to be able to sleep tonight
No one more loudly than her smile do I see
She'll be in my heart, she brought out the best in me.

I'll have a good cry and then take a look back
Look at all I have done and have a good laugh
forever I'll be, sad that she's gone
but that pain that's real is going into my songs

I'll no longer be treated like trash
Try to hurt me and I'll kick your ass.
I deserve more I deserve better
forgiveness and love bring us all together.

The Notes Will Tell You
Apr 13, 2009

I am searching for the key
its a mystery
A game she is playing with
me to get love for herself
So what do I do
How do I make you hear that
I love you

Scrambled eggs smell of burnt toast
memories are what will keep us close
Food spoiled rotten berries gone green
can help me to let go and finally scream
songs in my heart tears on my sleeve
the notes will tell you how I feel
The key lives in the door, no wonder you couldn't see
Truth and lies love is locked in between
Grounded by fear, governed by love
Through this door are stars above
Fences broken bricks all torn down
Sparkles float in every sound
faded and wasted, life, death and love
Sent you a message from a special dove
Souls drowning, spirits fading, green turning red
Sparkles and colour are needed to be fed.

I need Love so Badly
Apr 14, 2009

I need love so badly and it ain't coming from you
finding my way through the keyhole called life.
Go anywhere but here, just leave me alone.
There are other people who care
I don't wanna give up on you
but I do you have to find your own
way cause I don't give up on me.

Dream to Me
May 15, 2009

You are a dream to me
I open my eyes
It's you I see
Not far away.
but close in mind
close in heart
you are my dear
Forgiving eyes and
Loving arms
are all we need
to cleanse our mended
souls, our hearts
It won't take long
Forever is here
A word, a story from
long ago
Sticks in my mind
So I can remember
Why I ever cried
Amazing to see
all the possibilities
created by you
created by love
it's all we really need...
You really are a dream to me.

Burning with Desire
May 18, 2009

The smoke within
burning with desire
moves us forward
pawn to the last wire
we wait for love
We long for love
It emerges from our soul
Lifting us to new dimensions
Some place we've never been
But yet so familiar
We are born with our family
All together for times we cherish
We find it is us
We find we are love
Nothing can keep us away
We are here united
All because of you
Holding tight through all the blue
Looking ahead, looking away
the colours becoming brighter
than could ever be seen
The sun shines masks
of mirrors
Suddenly everything is clear
We smile, we laugh
We look at each other
We look at ourselves
Wondering what took us so long
Wondering what took us away
But we think of those days
To bring us back
To days of fun under the sun

Visible
May 19, 2009

Visible to me
what do others see
someone who is kind
lovable and purely free
why can't you see
you are beautiful
inside
if you just believe
a butterfly flying
along with the breeze
singing so gently
the trees do not utter a sound
they are astounded
that you have reached
solid ground
lifting your spirits
yet here you remain
tender and darling
your breath matches
sound.

Missing You
May 28, 2009

I miss you more than
you will ever know
I want you happy
I know you're in pain
I want to see you smile
and feel your hug again
To see joy in your eyes
will be the biggest surprise
no more tears that
shed down your face
only sunshine in
hurt is without a trace
sounds of the earth
will sing in delight
as you let go of fears
this special night
troubles gone, worries what's that
Love shines in and feels so warm
Love shines out after the storm.

Fallen From Grace
June 2009

Fallen from grace
I see my face
and know
that I want more
You don't love me
it's plain to see
to everyone except me
I look away from myself
my heart has fallen off the shelf
You left me crying
You left my lying
to myself
lonely and afraid
of who I can be
of the who that is me.

I see the light
it's waiting for me
the magic of night
is all that constructive
I don't care anymore
cause I want more.

And I want to change
my point of view
so that I see love
when I look at you.

Smiles I see happy
and free to live
and just be me.

Notes and sounds
keep haunting me
because it's your
face that I
long to see

somebody save
my life
I need love so
desperately

We Need Each Other
July 7th, 2009

Waiting, deserving fruit of the tree
hungry and craving all that we see
we want to be faithful
we all want to be loved
this is the time we pray above
a look to the left a look to the right
we march ahead we redeem our fight
battles to be won
love to be found
family and friends come soaring abound
dreams are for sharing
as is the love
we all need each other
to survive summer love.

Missing You
July 7, 2009

Missing you is harder than I thought
never thought I'd change my mind
from the hurt and the pain
to forgiveness and love
so strong it dominates my soul
so much I hope you know
I want you, I need you
you are like a drug to me
but only cause of the love
that I feel that will never
fade away
never fade away
my love for you
tears and sunshine
I take it all
just to have you
once again
please never fade away
cause I need you
you were never gone
just hidden by storm clouds
of misjudged actions and words
you were never gone
just lost in my world
of chaotic circles of storms
but I love you.

She Never Said the Words
Sept 9, 2009

She never said the words
harmful to my heart
but that is ok
she never said the words
that could heal my heart
but that is ok
wound is do deep
trying to fight
cheek to cheek
she never said the words
to let me know I'd
be all right
but that's ok
my heart is strong
she never said the words
but in my heart I'm fine
I may not believe it now
but cause she never said
the words
I know I have to
move ahead
I said the words
I hope I've healed
her soul
I said the words
to keep from being
torn apart
but torn apart
I feel cause she
never said the
words
I may not be OK

but have to believe that
time will heal
she never said the words
but that is ok
in my heart I'm
strong
and love is
never wrong.

I Already Know
Sept 13, 2009

Gotta give in some more
Gotta run to the shore
you see the way I look to you
just with your eyes
I already know
you came to me
you whispered
it was only me
this whole time
it was only you
do you hear me now
I'm a whisper in your ear
I'm your whole year
do you hear me now
I've always been you
you already know
you whispered in my ear
you told me to run
said time to have fun
you already knew
it was always you
I came round smiling
you whispered
do you hear me
now
I'm always here
always here...

Awaken
Sept 13, 2009

Awaken to the night
Awaken to the sounds
it's strange, I know
I never knew you were around
always felt a presence
didn't know it was you
it's strange I know
but I know you're true
awaken it's time
awaken you're mine
it's strange, it's true
I was always feeling blue
without music, without you
it's strange I know
not to hear a sound
that you were there
when I wasn't around
Awaken to the sounds
Awaken to the light
it's strange, it's true
it's strange I know
but I know you to be true.

Fear & Anger

"I let myself down and now I need to pick myself back up."

Gina R. Smith

Light and Dark
2008

Light and dark
no in between
can't see the difference
at least that's how
it seems

Forced to be a soldier
with no chance to dream
this is not living
I just want to scream

Hiding
Jan 7, 2009

Hiding away from what I can become
Not seeing the light
No energy to fight
hiding from fear the world has won

The Wind Lions Blow
Mar 27, 2009

the calendar is marked so I can remember all the years
each day that I've lived snarled, marked with fear
grasping for branches to reach to the top
the ground falls below but never do I stop

The lions keep roaring blowing wind in my eyes
and I spit out sand to my surprise

tasting like dust breathing for air
chocking on thoughts I scramble for prayer

god please help me from the wicked I see
God please help me to turn and fall safely
The colours I've seen are not what I've dreamed
I don't like them at all is what I screamed

My skin starts tingling my heart feels heat
I look down below and see lights underneath
I start climbing down not looking where I step
I keep my eyes focused on the souls that I've met

Greater than the ocean are sounds do I hear
Gently bringing me down their words are sincere
familiar faces stand with their arms stretched out wide
is the best feeling of love I could ever find.

Getting Stuck
Mar 29, 2009

Nobody knows where the hell I've been,
gonna make a fool of myself again.
Keep on getting stuck up in the same old scene
Baby why'd you have to go and be so mean.

Lost Souls
May 13, 2009

Bring us closer to make us whole
The shadows that creep
have no time to weep
as we frantically search
to renew our soul
Heaven forbid that we
should lose our soul
the worst thing we
could ever know
We come back together
and we rejoice with a smile
knowing we were here all the while
no rain on our parade
only laughter inside
we cry our eyes
for finding love inside
it's the best way to find
that piece of mind
passionate and free
beautiful are thee

Nothing to Fear
May 19, 2009

A new day, a new life
is set to begin
Today, Love is here
really is nothing to fear
We all have feelings
We are all full of love
no point running away
Doesn't get you anywhere
But more lost inside of your mind
Freedom lies in facing
all of our worst fears
when really there is
nothing to fear but fear itself.

Scared To Be Alone
May 19, 2009

Scared to be alone, crying when I sleep
scared that I may moan, scared that may weep
Questions being asked
Answers being given
Lead us to new days
Where the sun has already risen
Easy to see
Easy to recognize
Easy to make mistakes
Yet easy to overcome
Dive right in
and swim back up to the top
Forever you are here
the muddy waters have
Started to clear
A light is on the way
Brighter than the sun
knowing we are here
knowing we all are as one
never look away
Only look within
And love the skin you're in.

Fear is Just a Thought
May 22, 2009

Mind over mood
Fear is just a thought
our worst nightmares
it stops us in our spot

It keeps us from becoming
who we really are
it keeps us from shining
down upon the trees

Fear is not real
but real is who we are
Getting rid of fear
is to love within.

Feeling Anxious
May 23, 2009

Feeling so anxious
don't know where to turn
running around
I need to be found.

Shake Me to The Core
May 27, 2009

Anger shakes me from within
longing to be free
the shadows stare
trying to bring me down

but I will not let
them shake me sore
I only want peace
vibrating to my core

knock me, hit me
break me down
You will not win
I win the town

My soul is great
it's been put to the test
all I know is
I know I'm the best

The best in me
longing to be free
from past events
chains I do see

no longer held
I change my view
my hands are
clean
I am renewed

Little by Little
June 3, 2009

Little by little
the swan appears
little by little
we see our fears
holding our hands
a bow our heads
holding our hearts
inside instead
masks come off
Masks go on
Dreams say a lot
bring truth to the door
always searching
because we want more
trickling, pouring
release is near
peaceful calm
nothing to fear
dreams will come
true
anger is a chore
we have to think
to be angry
the hurt causes
the anger
I've been so
hurt in my
life that
is why
I am angry

Dark be Dark
June 10, 2009

Dark be dark
light be light
come forth to
show me
take out the
fright
locked in
my head
bring peace
instead
these mighty
forces
and eat
my bread

Too Many Worries
July 7, 2009

Too many worries on my mind
gotta shift the parallels of time
sleep must prevail
sound mind peaceful chains

whispers in the night
fade with sounds of
clay that haunt me
stop me from
resting my soul.

Angry Like Bees
Mar 14, 2009

There's so much anger as I dig for the truth
There's so much sadness as I lift off the roof
searching inside the answers I must find
I really need to open up my mind

hungry for love in all the wrong places
I wish I had her to hold me tight
I see her face but only in traces
this time has to be different it has to be right

I'm terribly sad today
I'm incredibly torn
whether or not to let you go
I don't want to forget the mother I know

hurt swarmed like bees
just won't leave me alone
I'm falling to my knees
I just want to go home

Scrambling to find the love I once had
because this life has turned bad
I'm angry I'm sad
I want the love I knew I once had.

I'm so torn whether or not to let you go
you once were there know you are gone
smiles, laughter, tears
it's just gone on too long.

mysterious you were but so am I
full of love but surrounded by fears

I can feel your hugs
I really want you here

rolling tears noise in my ears
I need someone to listen
to the heartache inside
cause it's you I'm missing

I want to do it my way
to make everything all right
tired of pretending you didn't leave us that night

I've been used an abused
and treated like trash
you threw me to the ground
and I shattered like glass

I'm still in shock that you left that night
I've wanted you there to kiss me goodnight
to tuck me in with my doll in hand
who got rid of my tears by holding her tight

I know I'm healing I can feel the heat on my head
I don't need you to guide me ahead
I choose to live my life without you instead
and I'll cherish my dreams as I go to bed.

I can't believe the change in my today
that girl yesterday this girl today
I'm bubbly and happy the girl I used to be
She's coming back fragments of me

Sometimes love is letting go of the
person you love the most
while keeping the memories
like cinnamon toast
keeping the memories that you love the most

Fighting the urge to eat
cause I want our eyes to meet
locked in an embrace
I really miss your face

I just want to hug everyone and hold them tight
love them so dearly and squeeze with all my might
I have so much love for this entire world
all because of that little girl.

Why can't people just learn to love
instead of tearing it all apart
what are we so afraid of
we all need each other we all need love

Without love you've got nothing, nothing at all
you die inside cry rivers in your mind
we all need lover to keep us together
without love we all just crumble and fall.

Anger Turned Inward
Mar 15, 2009

Anger turned inward does nothing at all
just feeds self destruct and self esteem too
rapid with fear instinct to run to any love near
but I will not be a victim because of your fears

I just don't know how to get angry enough
I just want to run from place to place
until I go home forever
I have to find a way not to blame you anymore
and skip ahead on to my life
I'm tired of waiting that you'll come back to me
But how in the world do I say goodbye to you?

I'm tired of missing what we used to have
because there's a wall in between
made of the hardest of bricks
it's a situation that I just cannot fix.

Enough of You, Time for Me
Mar 2009

That is who I was and this is who I
became spring is here it is time to change
I ripped up all your pictures one by one
then I brought my spirit with me and went for a run.

time to live my life again
time to have some fun
soak in all the sunshine
because it is all mine

washing my hands clean
from all the dirt from you
cleaning dust from the attic
that trapped me inside of you

anger exercise sobbing
blown like the wind moving with the rhythm
and jumping stomping at end

The house being and feeling so
empty! That is how she left me
feeling inside.
The empty house left me feeling empty
inside.

Gone was the girl with the superstar dreams
left was someone ripped at the seams

What I'm Worth
Apr 18, 2009

I know what I'm worth
not a damn penny to you
I know what I'm worth
its diamonds to me.

Feel to Heal
Aug 20, 2009

Let me feel what I need to feel
Let me heal how I need to heal
You are not me, you do not know my pain
So judge me not I am not insane
I hurt, I cry, I bleed, I ache
I sob, I tremble, I run, I shake
you think you know what I have
been through I'll tell you this you
know nothing and do not want to be where I have been
I can teach, I can show the marks
on my skin
only then can you imagine where I have been
If you will not listen then ridicule
me not.
If you will not listen then do not even ask
If you will not listen I will not teach
I have much to offer if you will
only let me try....

Watched Like a Hawk
Aug 21, 2009

Made to feel worse instead of
better is no way to heal
being watched like a hawk
with every gawk
makes me want to puke
and to scream
leave me be
let me see
let me free
don't lock me in
and tie me down
don't turn me into someone who is not me
I scream to you all to just let me be me
that is how I will be free

They All Know
Aug 20, 2009

They all think they know
me but what do they know?
I scream
I shout
oh my God
heaven forbid that I should shout
and show emotion?!

Pain

"Sitting in silence does no good at all, we need to talk about what happened or I do at least. I need to get out the pain to heal"

Gina R. Smith

Never Used to Be This Way
Jan 7, 2009

I never used to be so angry
I never used to be so sad
No longer can I live this way
always being mad
its time to live and time to shine
no longer will I whine.

Struggled
Jan 7, 2009

I've struggled to find love
never could find my way
always someone stupid
who has to have their say

Driven by emotion
I feel alive enough to die
but wanting to feel passion
makes me ill, weak and I cry

Long Winter
Feb 2009

I really did love you
you misinterpreted my silence
as being crazy
when really all I could
think about was you

didn't want to think
about anything else
cause you were so
sweet on my mind

But now all that is ruined
I've lost my real love
now winter will go
on for far too long

Don`t Want to Breathe
Feb 2009

I'm just sitting here in silence thinking
of what a mess I've made
don't want to breathe
don't want to sing
I need to start over again
I need to begin

Breaking Down to the Core
Feb 2009

I'm starting to welcome the silence and not the noise
its ok to say it's too much for today
I don't want anyone to really look at me
cause then they will see all of this pain
the only way out is to go in

The girl in the river just wants to go home
all of this has just been me trying to find my way
find my way out and to find my way in

I have to believe & I have to have faith

sitting here in traumatic shock realizing what is
really real hasn't felt real at all
it's been wicked and cruel
I'm seeing who I really am and breaking
down to the core
I don't want to face what I really have to face

My brain keeps going in circles trying to
make sense of what is all going on
translucent feelings and a zombie like state
sentences full of stutters and rambles
the jigsaw is scrambling together one piece at a time

but I'm climbing the ladder of true reality
love is the calming factor that will lead me to bliss
it's just all my life that I really really miss
have to make up for lost time
I think that's the only way that I will be fine

who has really been there for me in my time of need

people think that it's easy but it ain't
easy at all I've tried so hard not to fall
my head feels clouded full of too much pain
thanks to you I'm nothing but stained.

This is me and this is how it is
if you don't like what you see
then maybe you really don't understand me

I have a lot to give and a lot to learn
I want to know you I want to know me
I'm jumping and twisting all between the lines
looking inside and not falling behind

Misunderstood
Feb 2009

I feel so all alone
and no one understands
the kind of pain I am in
I just want to let the love in

looking for answers
to the journey of my life
knocking on doors
someone provide me some relief

nervous and scared
don't want to be alone
I need to be hugged
I need to be loved

why can't someone see into my soul
see what I'm missing
see the girl underneath
maybe only I can provide my own relief

running and jumping
the trees are in my way
searching for that open path
gotta find it before I crash

Wound That Never Heals
Feb 2009

The wound that never heals
it's ok to be sad
it's ok to be mad
but it's not ok to be treated bad.

Loss and Healing
Feb 2009

It's always going to be there I guess
the memory of it all
just take the pain away
cause I no longer want to feel small
fitting in the pieces
one step at a time
crying a lot
and healing my mind.

Tears Under Lock & Key
Feb 2009

Everything really hurts I can't believe how messed
up I got. I know I'm getting better but it really
is extremely painful but I choose to be free
so many tears locked away for so many years
boiling anger and raging fears
turned nights into days and days into
nights just going through the motions
of my tortured life

Need to express all my fears and concerns
need to escape to freedom that's all I know
running doesn't help the rain builds up inside
Until I'm drowning in my talented mind

Everything daddy could no longer see
The girl I was and longed to be
Escape to freedom that's all I know
longed for the moment to let the emotions flow
I'm purging my soul from the rage inside
escaping to freedom to find my peace of mind.

I Give Up On You
Feb 2009

I need to let myself out
I need to be free from all of this
it hurts so much oh what did I do
I needed so much love from you

my stomach is ill from figuring it all out
my mind is frantic wandering all about
give me some peace and happiness too
all I ever wanted was to be loved by you

you've torn me all apart
is there anything left of me
just want to go back to very start
just want to let my mind be free

It's not fair that I've had to feel this way
I need so much love and care
I feel like you've blown me away
and there's nothing left to repair

so much I want and have wanted to do
you left us you took me you threw me away
what the hell was I supposed to do?!
fragile and small but so much I want to say

A story to tell
I know it well
hidden so deep
which makes me weep

sweet turned to sorrow
love turned to hate

hop turned to shame
nothing left but rain

that is what happened
now I can see
felt so trapped
I'm finally free

I have to love myself
to let real love in
I wonder what would have happened
if none of this had happened

Its You
Mar 12, 2009

the others they can rot in hell if they don't like me
I don't care cause it's you I needed love from
it's from you I needed care
letting go is gonna take a bit
but only cause of how hard I've been hit

Fuel to the Fire
Mar 13, 2009

I keep adding more fuel to the fire
searching for love in all the wrong places
I need to unwind my mind
untangle all the strings
that got tied up into knots
no longer will I be fragile and distraught

My brain just hurts
from all your thoughts and fears
don't take my words
and put them in your thoughts
that's not selfish to say

so much loss felt like I had been tossed
flung around so hard curled up like lard
folding into pieces hiding in the creases

Happy Pills
Mar 2009

Happy pills don't take the hurt away
they take the snarls and lock them all away
you're stuck inside and can't have your say
you find yourself gone your heart turned to clay

Just Want to Back to Before That Day
Mar 14, 2009

I got picked on a lot cause I was different than others
and all I wanted was love from my mother
but she disappeared and left me with screams
I felt like no one really loved me
as that's what it seems

I've searched for the truth my entire life long
why we melt into pieces and cannot stay strong
love holds us in and shuts out the pain
it lets us know the grace we have gained

I'm clouded with emotion
never ending it seems
gotta wash it all away
I don't like what I've seen

I ran into a wall
I've been hit by bricks
will someone just end
all of these painful tricks.

I just want to go back to before
that awful day
where the sun was shining
and the colours were bright
back to home where I felt no fright.

Remain Calm at the Scene
Mar 22, 2009

I feel sick inside and twisted like roots
all because of what I once knew
pain inside that was hidden so deep
memories of you I had no clue

Trying to remain calm at the scene
twisted and torn all in a dream
running from fire running to the cage
inside of these I throw all my rage

longing to feel the wind in my hair
I grab my breathe and toss it in the air
swirling like leaves from the trees in the fall
I am seeing myself thru the brick wall

Green and blue and turquoise and pink
colours flow everywhere above and beneath
stars that shine brighter the sun so hot
I am finished with being who I am not.

Lights go up and lights go down
smiling and happy sad with a frown
not feeling right not feeling ok
heal my heart take the hurt all away.

Waste of Time
Mar 2009

Working out is a waste of my time
hard I work but impatient I grow
need more time to invest my mind
to be creative with all I know.

Tired of Lies
Mar 24, 2009

I can feel the tears behind my eyes
full of truth and tired of lies
stars falling twirling like the leaves
change is a coming cause that's what I need.

Can Survive Without Her
Mar 2009

I don't need her to be better
I can survive without her haunting me
keep her in my heart
keep all the good memories

Damage is Done
Apr 7, 2009

It's just too late
the damage is done
but don't you worry
because I have won

Hid the Best Part of Me
Apr 13, 2009

So much trauma before I was a teen
So young to see what she had done to me.
I went and hid the best part of me.
Worms in my heart and all through my skin.
I couldn't find my way back in.
the sore is so far I used to say
on the horizon I see today.
Storm is brewing getting full of steam
Flashing lights are all I see
Wind soars my heart up past the
clouds to a beautiful vision
pink blue purple green.

Wounded So Deep
May 16, 2009

How could I not
be with you that night
you took away my life
you took away my soul
I cried for hours
I cried for days
No Medication can take
away that pain
Wounded so deep
All I do is sleep
The music brings comfort
When I am missing you
When it hurts so much
it really does cleanse my soul
Tears stream down
As I say goodbye to you
Rolling down my cheek
As I say hello to me
But I'll always be here
In spirit, heart and mind
Locked far away
Happy times I will never forget
To keep my heart nourished
To keep my heart loved
When I need to remember
Where it is that I come from.

Fragmented Heart
May 2009

Fragmented heart
torn into pieces
from all of the tears
of my life
fighting to live
fighting to die
all
because of
questions of why
sad little girl
with love in
her heart
wants the
torture
to stop
tearing her apart...

Follow the Rules
May 2009

It doesn't make sense that life can be so cruel
but I know in my heart that we have to follow the rules

So many people living without a home
let's open our hearts because they are our own
we need to be strong
we need to open our arms
Look into the sky for strength, that way we can't go wrong

My heart has so many tears that i cannot even cry
with so much devastation
I really wonder why
why have so many people been given so much grief
and why are we just sitting instead of providing love and relief?!

Give into your hearts and you'll give in to this world
there's truth inside our hearts
and even more inside our minds

Can't Describe This Feeling
May 23, 2009

Can't describe this feeling
inside
it rips me apart
it tears my soul
but now I know
I've found what
I stole
I found the strength
to fight to the top
without giving in to hate
I have found my place
I have found my home.

So much has happened
so much emotion inside
begging to be free
my soul is begging
to cry to me

It's coming forth
it's coming soon
one day is here
one day is how
we find the fix
we find our hearts
beneath the sticks.

Pain is Too Much
May 30, 2009

The pain is too much to bear
All I want to do is
let down my hair
singing a song
where everyone
sings along
marching and waving
out to the world
where have you been
they shout and sing
waiting for the
fun to really begin
I know you're there
smiling and waiting
while you're still scared
but I am here
we are all here
to catch you
without pain
soon you'll see
what surprises
are really meant
to be
the world is here
you are there
come join hands
together we stand.

Tired and Frail
May 31, 2009

Tired and frail
no use fighting
the tears that need
to fall from the sky
no one will hurt you
or question why
they just see your pain
and want you to lie
they long for your smile
and the love that
you give.

Take a few moments
to find the space within
you'll see the love
shining in.

all for you
and all for love
you will fly free
as a dove.

Emotion we Feel Helps Us Heal
May 31, 2009

It's emotion we feel
that helps us to heal
our heart beats fast
cause we are scared within
yet feeling so great
will let us in
Don't want to cry
don't want to feel
just want pain gone
that is so surreal
Anger that hurts
it stunts our growth
Shaking inside
to free our mind.

Painted by Hate
June 6, 2009

Painted by hate
stuck in between
is this really
my fate
sliding away
can't face the pain
locked inside
can't chase
my mind
to see
the brighter
lit day

Silence is Deafening
June 22, 2009

Silence is deafening
but also music to
my ears
anxious thoughts
from all of those years
thinking of love
thinking of rain
want to escape
from all of this pain.

Lost & Confused
June 2009

Lost, confused
nothing in between
colours of leaves
I cannot see
wind going one way
charged to the next
wonder why I can't
see that I am the best
Frightened to see
the stars in the sky
no one believes
the truth in me
slanted to the ground
not to be found
upwards we look
and open all the books.

Lack of Emotion
June 25, 2009

Lack of emotion
blunted by truth
taken away
no where to turn
but to look above
look within
see the light
surround the pale moon
that is howling to be free..

Hurt
June 2009

Listen to me
take me seriously
when I say I hurt
When I say there
is trouble
a problem
I follow my gut
stand up for truth
try not to hurt
I choose love
but to heal
real problem needs
addressing.

Torn Apart From Anxious Thoughts
July 9, 2009

Torn apart from anxious thoughts
want it to disappear like storm
clouds clearing
sun coming out to shine upon
the smiles of those who
abound with love to all
human beings and creatures alike
heart pounding just want to
cry let it all out so that
I can find my peace
within
it can be so easy if
people would just believe
stand up fight for
what you want don't
take advice that
doesn't feel right
only way to have a
peaceful night.

No One Should Have to be Alone
July 16, 2009

No one should have to be alone
no one should ever have to moan
listening to sharks eat you in the night
drowning your place full of fright
no place in this world for
heartache and pain
trying to break free from
all of the chains
listening to you is blessings from above
holding my hand our entrance is grand
we march we follow we lead we wing
hoping to bring peace within

Sitting in Silence
Aug 22, 2009

Sitting in silence
does no good at all
we need to talk
about what happened
or I do at least
I need to get out
the pain to heal

Despair

"part of me just wants to die, tired of life, tired of everyone's lies."
Gina R. Smith

Dark Eyes
2008
dark eyes are

my state of mind
no one to help me
no one to care
there's a reason to
love when you're feeling
fine but where I'm at
feels lonely inside
I try so hard to get
through it all
but I keep falling backwards
I'm on the brink.

Horrible World
2008

I need to find peace
in this horrible horrible
world. I'm so far gone, I've
fallen behind. Please help me
to find a state of bliss cause
I really feel I am losing my mind
I need some help I need someone
to care. I need to feel calm
I wish I had a mom.

Setting Myself up for Heartbreak
2008

Why do I fall for people I can't have
I set myself up for heartbreak
I have to stop doing this to myself
I have to learn to heal without doing myself harm
I'm so tired of living in misery all I want to do is scream
I've got to find my happiness cause I really want to live
Just can't live like this I don't call this living, not at all
I want my freedom to express who I am
Acting and singing and writing all the time
I need to do this to satisfy my soul
I feel so hungry for the party
anorexic without my dreams
purging and purging the emotion is not a dream
gotta express all these feelings
someway somehow

Lost my Dream
2009

Why do I keep falling out of my dream
not knowing what to do I just don't have a clue
my eyes are misty
can't even see
wish someone would look and see the real me
I've waited so long for my dream to begin
living and learning and screaming again
feeling pretty hopeless I guess I've lost my dream
sitting here staring, feeling pretty numb
people don't see me as special only as dumb
Tired, so tired can't live like this anymore
Fighting the sorrow keep trying to grow

So Much Heartache
Feb 2009

You caused me so much heartache
you caused me so much pain
you've made me fucking crazy
I've really gone insane

Don't know how you did it
but you somehow found a way
can't take this life I'm living
time to throw it all away

Time to actually live my life
the one I'm meant to live
I really have so much love
that I'd really love to give.

Feel So Lost
Feb 2009

I feel so lost
I don't know what to do
tired of crying
tired of feeling blue

I want to feel happy
I want to feel the sky
get rid of the anxiety
stop asking why

Lie of Coping
Feb 2009

caught in the lie of coping with her life
I've been suffering way too long
It's time to end it and set me free
I may be little but I am strong
I'll find my wings and ride out this storm

Just Put Up With It
Feb 2009

I just put up with it
I just put up with everything
and now I've had enough
so much anger that needs to disappear
I need to get rid of all my fears
put an end to all these tears
so long oh God how did I cope
I know that I'm at the end of my rope
Time to dissipate and time to set free
the girl inside I've always dreamed to be
I really really cannot wait to be me
it really is the time to set me free

struggling and hoping
crying and coping
strength turned to weakness
pain turned to shame
are all these people really blame

I deserved better but I treated myself worse
letting these guys whip me like a horse
all because I never opt to be
from who I needed it the most
all because of love
when I needed it the most

I'm looking inside and I'm struggling with the pain
blood and tears inside every single vein
I'm struggling inside to find my peace of mind
trying to find happiness a smile not to hide

slowly and surely it's starting to appear

in very small doses with every single tear
happiness I've not felt in very many years
trust takes the sadness and makes it disappear

my eyes are irrelevant to what people really see
no one really ever understands me
even know I'm really only starting to see
the girl inside that really is me
and wants to be set free.

don't feel like putting on that happy face
I feel it's always just a waste
I need to have a pure true smile
something that's been hidden a very long while

I'm starting to heal cause I let myself feel
all the hurt inside and accept it as real
everything's raw everything's truth all the real deal
even bare boned to every single meal

So pretend to let it all out
it's what I've been longing to scream about
jumping with joy jumping with anger
no longer will I have to feel like a stranger

headache so deep right down into my core
brain thinking hard then thinking it some more
trying to remember all the closed doors
drugged like feeling thoughts are paralyzed more

distorted distracted disgusted with shame
dreams that were shattered mom is to blame
trying to remember and tired of this game
I've gotta remember where all the happiness was stained

Fighting so hard to come to the truth
learning so much what's underneath

coping with strength and coping with fear
I'm trying so hard to look in the mirror

End to end and piece by piece
looking on top and looking beneath
only seeing Capitals and alphabets
mixed up emotions and blood hurdling grief

I'm being yanked and torn so tired of being worn
like a piece of old clothing or a person being mourned
knocking and knocking on every single door
looking for the answers because I want more

I want more life then there is even to give
maybe it's why I've managed so long to even live
I am still wondering what I ever did
I was only 11 I was only a kid

stomach is churning my chest is burning
searching so hard I am still learning
no longer purging my thoughts are merging
living and learning loving and yearning

nervous and shaking so scared of what's inside
trembling from what I've tried so hard to hide
I still can't see it's really bothering me
I've got to know I've got to be free

Shaken and torn I think I need to mourn
Lost dazed bewildered confused reborn
Thoughts running eyes blinking from too much thinking
Thirsty cold think things are linking

Tired of Living That Way
Mar 2009

Need good memories in order to let go
forget all the bad you don't need to know
keep the good ones in order to grow
so you can have that world you've always known

I was not tired of living just tired of living that way
my mind was tortured because you left that day
so had to believe that you shattered my world
and left me alone as a little girl

That matters no more I am gaining control
all the torture will soon be rolling down the hall
Marbles gone wild rivers and streams
I want my life back I want to live my dreams.

Just want to drift out to sea
where no one can really see me
all because you left me to cry
all because I don't know why

The Vessel
Mar 2009

The vessel is long and the vessel is clean
the horn began to sound and my heart turned green
all around me were strangers that I knew
they stood all around us it was me and you.

running to the basement where I hear screams
it is there where I long to find my dreams
shattering like glass letting the water surpass
surprised by the strength in the difficult class
wood house on fire with stairs with Kathleen
climbing up with a motorcycle to the one sobbing

Looking down looking up again
seeing time change the history
of the between of you and me.

Final Knot
Apr 13, 2009

I want to be alone, curl up and die
someone please just let me cry
can't turn the handle
the faucet is hot, please let me
untwist the final knot.

I'll Hold On
Apr 13, 2009

I'm having bad thoughts
please make the go away
thoughts of giving up
because I don't know
how to end the pain

I'll hold on to hope
I'll hold on to faith
I'll keep fighting hard
I'll keep stars in my mind.

So tired now drowning so deep
months its been since I've had
peaceful sleep
Ready to live ready to die
someone help find a
way to cry.

Want my happy ending
it is what I deserve
Fought like the bull
to just keep on living

Tired of Running
May 14, 2009

I want my parents to see me happy.
I don't want them to see me hurting anymore.
I know that I have to save myself.
I wrote before, I will forever be old.
I want to be ok.
I want everything to be all right,
don't want to be angry and crying every night.
I gotta give in to myself.
I gotta treat myself right.
So tired of running
pretending everything's all right.
It hurts too much don't
wanna fell like this no more.
Just wanna walk in and
close that ugly door.
Room for me to breath and to
live my life again.
Room for me to din to sing
it all from my soul.
Loving and giving are the traits
of me. Will keep me strong as
I fall onto my knees.
I need to keep the faith while
searching for my truth.
I really want to live to sing
from roof to roof
Smiling from within is how
it will begin.
To open up my heeart knowing
me from within.
Gotta reach for those stars
That are so sweet to me

Gotta reach out for the top
My soul will never stop
Love is in my soul more than
you and I could ever know.
But tears keep holding me back.
from dancing in my soul
time is precious and the time
is finally near.
Where I will sit and cry all
Those haunting tears
Then They'll turn to laughter
and then some happy tears
no longer will I feel all those
angry fears.
Jumping to the moon, over and
beyond. Landing in the sun
and smiling happy yawns.
Breaking free from danger
Breaking free from old restraints
Breathing deep within myself
Living starts again.

Feeling Broken
May 16, 2009

Feel broken and destructive
Inside my lonely heart
waiting for the time
when the pain finally ends
can't take it anymore
don't want to fall
onto the muddy floor.
Need to escape
from inside my
tortured mind
It's time to stop
This game that
we've created
It's time to shut down
Those ugly darned thoughts
because we are beautiful
We know that this is true
I love you deep
We know that this is true
It's time to breathe
life inside our hearts
Loving completely free
To live the best in me
Got to show to the world
That love surpasses all
We all can heal
We just have to feel
All those ugly thoughts
Face our thoughts and fears
That have haunted us
over the past, over the years
Nothing to hide.

We have life inside
Growing taller with
Self respect, self love
we all need love we all breathe life
Time has come
time is here
Soon we'll be grinning
from ear to ear
Listen to what I say
Today is Love, Love is today.

Room With a View
May 21, 2009

Don't want no room with a
window view
want to be outside with nature
and with you
Want to breath the clean fresh air
Don't want to smoke in despair
want control over my thoughts
Don't want to waste
what I have got
Want to live more than I wish to die
Gotta keep saying "If only I try"
Don't want it to be hard
want it all to come easy
Playing games isn't fun
if you don't have the sun
Want to know what is wrong
To correct what is right
Don't want to give in
I do wanna fight
Life is worth the risk
to take chances if you dare
Gotta keep on trying
to repair all the tears
One, two, three,
are wishes that I grant
For me and for you
For everyone around
Take it today
Live for today
Live with all of your might
You'll soon see, it's' worth the fight.

Feeling the Pressure
May 22, 2009

Feeling the pressure
Feeling the heat
I won't give in
To any defeat
I wish to grow
I wish to love
I wish on stars
that shine above
crystal clear, mirror of my soul
haunting my heart
I need to caress my soul
I need to find the rhythm inside
For that will plant seeds
inside of my mind
Got to give in but yet not give up
Got to keep on track
the tracks I do jump
Breathing the air
Breathing in life
I know I've found
light in the dark.

Day Passes By Darker
May 22, 2009

Each day passes by
Darker it seems
when really I'm
left with only my dream
Chances turned to fate
get rid of all the hate.

Masking the Hurt
May 30, 2009

Drugs just mask
all the hurt inside
Doctors' orders
cause they don't care
they think they are
Smart
when really they are not.
I know the truth
I want to sing it off the roof
no longer alive
I am dead inside
all because drugs are in my eyes
Dreams are lost
What do I care
I just look in the mirror
It's a zombie that stares.

No One Listens
May 30, 2009

No one cares
no one listens
birds fly by
it's them I'm missing
Just let me fall
so I don't see
the sky
Then everyone will
be asking why
why she didn't
live her dreams
cause they put
me on drugs
ripped me apart
at the seams
the colours are gone
never coming back
I fall down on my face
No one heard it go splat.

Looking For Answers
June 3, 2009

Looking for the answers
I do not give up on faith
I trust where I am going
even though I don't have a life
I know where I've been
or have I really been there
before
Looking for answers
I do not give up hope
even when the drugs
bring me to the end
of my rope
I hold on tight to
see the eyes
of animals delight
watching as I go
down the path
I chose to go
the path I chose
to find the
answers where
mysteries lie
rocky and ridden
from circles in
my mind
come to clean
we find where
we've been
looking for answers
to all that we've
seen we keep
our hearts locked

up where they
belong.

Yearning and Churning
June 6, 2009

Yearning and churning to
find my way
believing in magic
truth I scream to say

it really is real
and I just have
to believe
that I can
make it
through
this
day.

Bullet Meets the Horn
June 6, 2009

Bullet meets the horn
no life left to live
too sensitive for this
giving in to death
my life is not fair
let go of me
see me go
I told you all
see me go
watch me go
I go now

Don't Feel The Flame
June 8, 2009

Tired don't feel the flame
no one to blame
but am going insane
don't know which way to turn
Left is drought right is sour
nothing seems right anymore
do you follow your heart
is anyone there
you know God is there
but no one seems to care
can't find my way
just want to have my say
Leaves are scattered
from the summer storm
rain fallen down
soaking my mind's ground

No One Can Save Me
June 8, 2009

No one can save me now
I've tried everything
to no avail
So angry and hurt inside
restless from the drugs
can't even play a song
non one listens except
for God but people
call me crazy
When I'm not
so I give in
I give up the fight
no breath left
no light inside
lights out for
me.

Beautiful Goodbye
Aug 2, 2009

Beautiful goodbye
with beautiful sounds
sends me shivers
with light all around
Beautiful goodbye
with the people that i love
surrounded by faith
and God above
Beautiful goodbye
with peace in my heart
no more tears
but stars in my heart
Beautiful goodbye
is all i know
blessed for life by sadness i
know
Beautiful goodbye
with sounds of
music the love
of my life
i feel they
are gone forever
Beautiful goodbye
with wind in
your hair
i want to know
are you really there?
Beautiful goodbye
to a world i once
knew
happy and free
why can't that be me?

All Alone
Aug 21, 2009

all alone
no one who
really cares
no one understands
why i need to cry
shameful as sin
to have a tear
on my chin
how dare you
challenge my
fears with
all of your tears
is what she heard
them all say
all alone
no one understands
why i need to scream
how dare you fall
apart at the seams
how dare you let
us see the pain
we all are in
she could hear
them all say
all alone
all by myself
i sit here
and stare
i sit here
and cringe
anxious
within

as no one
will let
the tears
spill out
onto my chin
so
i sit here
all alone
hold it
all in
till my head
pops off
gets lost
forever
lost
within

Summers Over
Aug 28, 2009

Summer's almost over
I wanted to be saved
but I don't feel saved
at all
feel dragged down
don't know
who I am
barely knew
summer
but it knew
me
haunted by drugs
driven by fear
left alone
to drown
in my tears.

Summer of Suicide
Aug 29, 2009

summer of suicide
summer of hate
can't even fathom what I ate
what happened to love
what happened to fate
I needed you
I needed to believe
the light between
you and I
is stronger than
any thought
that comes our
way
drugs that kill
the spirit inside
dying to find
it inside of my mind
without you
don't know where I'd
be
all I know
is I'm thankful for love
thankful for the day
wishing on stars to
find my way through
darkened nights
feeling the sun
giving me thoughts
of hope
that one day
a cloud will just be a
a cloud

not a darkened
dream that
frightens me
to the covers
not sending me
away with
tears full of shivers
I needed you
I needed to believe
the light between
you and I is really
all I needed to
believe.

Tired and Worn
Sept 14, 2009

Tired and worn
searching for our home
we are broken glass
trying to look beyond
view blocked
searching for our home
tired and worn
God please don't
don't give up on me
trembling with leaves
fallen to the ground
finding our truth
to find our way home.

When You Can Hardly Walk

When you can hardly walk
when you can hardly run
you know you're missing
all the fun
When you can hardly breathe
and just want to leave
you know you are worth
fighting for
missing the life
missing the dreams
we just want love
like that of ice cream
when your smile has faded
and your thoughts are jaded
you know you've fallen
to the floor
When you can't see the light
When you can't see the stars
you know your
dreams are made
for more.

Where Am I
Sept 17, 2009

Where am I
here nor there
longing to play
in the sun
longing for love
to surround my soul
take away the fear
from it all
where am I
but lost in between
stuck in a place
no one wants to see
imagine a void
so deep in your head
imagine a house
all torn apart
where am I
but lost within
wanting to be free
so that I can see
surrender your heart
surrender your soul
it will take you places
you'd never know
key to life is
playing the game
finding you're strong
through all the pain.
Where am I
but a love that
never dies
asleep, buried

hibernating like
a bear but once
spring comes the
smiles will flow

Prologue

Gina is an angel now, she is teaching the other angels to sing. There is no one more qualified to be a guardian angel. Maybe she'll look out for you one day.